Pirate Percy's Parrot

by Sheila May Bird

illustrated by Luke Flowers

OXFORD
UNIVERSITY PRESS
AUSTRALIA & NEW ZEALAND

OXFORD
UNIVERSITY PRESS

Oxford University Press is a department of the University of Oxford.
It furthers the University's objective of excellence in research, scholarship,
and education by publishing worldwide. Oxford is a registered trademark
of Oxford University Press in the UK and in certain other countries.

Published in Australia by
Oxford University Press
Level 8, 737 Bourke Street, Docklands, Victoria 3008, Australia

First published 2015
This edition 2019
Reprinted 2021, 2022

ISBN 9780190317577

Series Advisor: Nikki Gamble
Designed by Fiona Lee, Pounce Creative
Illustrated by Luke Flowers
Printed in Singapore by Markono Print Media Pte Ltd

Chapter 1
Polly the Parrot

Pirate Percy had a parrot called Polly.

Pirate Percy loved Polly, and Polly loved Pirate Percy.

One-eyed Jack had a beautiful ship.
It had a tall mast, a big sail and a flag.
Pirate Percy's ship didn't.

One-eyed Jack had a HUGE chest
full of treasure. Pirate Percy didn't.

But Pirate Percy had Polly, his parrot.
Pirate Percy loved Polly more
than anything.

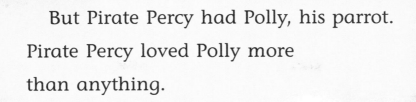

Pieces of eight,
pieces of eight!

He loved the way she sat
on his shoulder and squawked.

One-eyed Jack didn't have a parrot.
He didn't even have a budgie.
"Arrr, it's no good being a pirate
if you haven't got a parrot to sit on
your shoulder," growled One-eyed Jack.

He looked at his beautiful ship with its tall mast.
He looked at the big sail and the flag. He looked at all
the gold and jewels in his huge treasure chest and shouted,

"I WANT A PARROT!"

Chapter 2
Parrot Overboard!

One night there was a terrible storm. But pirates are good at sleeping. They can even sleep through **crashing** thunder and **howling** winds.

While Pirate Percy and his pirates were asleep, a big wave swept Polly over the side of the boat.

The following day, the sun came out. The pirates had no idea there had been a storm.

The pirates realised Polly was missing. They looked and looked, but they couldn't find Polly anywhere.

Pirate Percy was very worried. He sobbed into his handkerchief. Then he blew his nose noisily.

"Poor, poor, Polly. Whatever has happened to her?"

One-eyed Jack and his pirates had slept through the terrible storm, too. Now they were enjoying the warm sunshine.

Parrot ahoy!

Suddenly, a pirate spotted Polly from the crow's nest.

Polly's cage was bobbing
about on the sea.

One-eyed Jack became very excited.
"A parrot, a parrot – just what I want!"
He fished Polly out of the sea
and took her to his cabin.

One-eyed Jack took
a good look at Polly.

"Arrr, this is Polly,
Pirate Percy's parrot!
Now she can sit
on my shoulder, arrr!"

But Polly didn't like
One-eyed Jack. And she didn't
want to sit on his shoulder at all.
She bit his ear and chewed the
buttons off his coat.

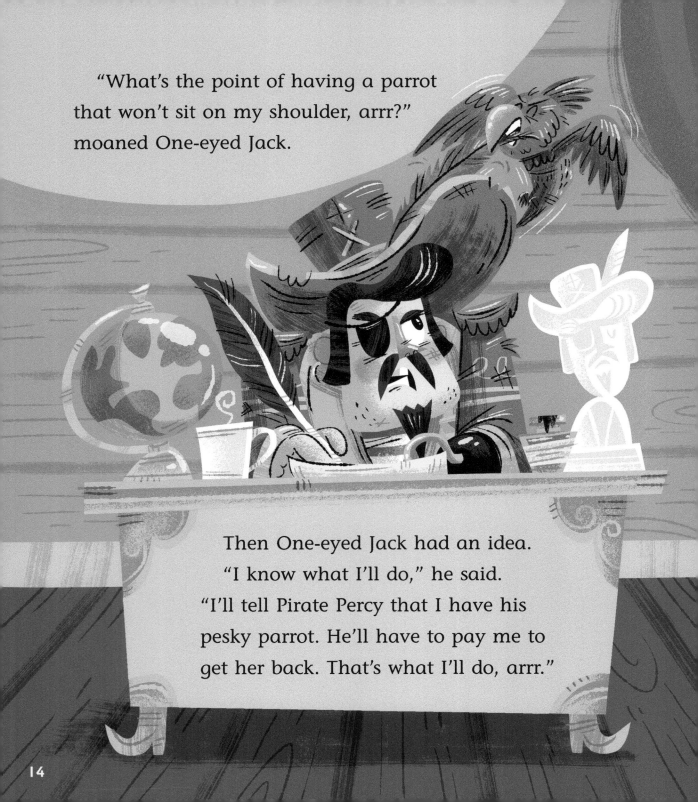

"What's the point of having a parrot that won't sit on my shoulder, arrr?" moaned One-eyed Jack.

Then One-eyed Jack had an idea. "I know what I'll do," he said. "I'll tell Pirate Percy that I have his pesky parrot. He'll have to pay me to get her back. That's what I'll do, arrr."

He wrote a note in his very best handwriting.

Dear Pirate Percy,

I've got your parrot. I'll keep her until you pay me 1000 gold coins.

1000 gold coins or Polly walks the plank, arrr.

Best wishes,
One-eyed Jack

One-eyed Jack put the note in a bottle, sealed it with a cork and threw it into the sea.

Chapter 3
Polly on the Loose

Percy missed Polly sitting on his shoulder. He missed her squawking, "Pieces of eight, pieces of eight!"

Bottle ahoy!

Pirate Percy read the note.
"*1000* gold coins!" he exclaimed.

He looked in his treasure chest.
It was almost empty. What was
he going to do?

Back on One-eyed Jack's ship, Polly flew about the cabin, spilling drinks and breaking things. The more the pirates tried to catch her, the more mess they made.

One-eyed Jack wrote another note.

Pirate Percy,

Pay me 500 gold coins for Polly.

500 gold coins or we'll be having roast parrot for dinner, arrr.

One-eyed Jack

He put the note in a bottle, sealed it with a cork and threw it into the sea.

Bottle ahoy!

Pirate Percy read the note.
"*500* gold coins!" he cried.

The treasure chest was still almost empty.
The pirates looked in their money boxes.
They were empty too, except for two plastic
buttons and a pebble.

Pirate Percy was very, very worried
about Polly. He paced up and down
the deck. It made the boat rock.

Polly was having great fun on One-eyed Jack's ship.
She made some of the pirates walk the plank.

Polly sat on One-eyed Jack's head.
She gripped his head so tightly
that she gave him a headache.

One-eyed Jack wrote another note.
His handwriting was not his best.

Pirate Percy,

I'll take 50 gold coins for your
parrot. That's not a lot to ask
for the safe return of your bird.

arrr, OW!
One-eyed Jack

One-eyed Jack put the note in a bottle,
sealed it with a cork and threw it into the sea.

Chapter 4
Pockets Full of Fluff

Bottle ahoy!

Pirate Percy read the note.

"*50* gold coins!" he said. The pirates looked in their pockets. They were empty except for a half-eaten toffee and some fluff.

Pirate Percy sucked the toffee and thought.

"It seems to me, me hearties, that we might not have to pay for Polly after all," he said.

They waited for another bottle with another note.

TREASURE

That night Polly sat on One-eyed Jack's
hammock and sang a boring song.
It was a very, *very* boring song.

The next day, some of One-eyed Jack's pirates fell overboard when Polly flew by, squawking RIGHT IN THEIR EARS!

Who's a naughty pirate then?

One-eyed Jack wrote another note.

Please, PLEASE, Pirate Percy,

You can have your parrot back.
I will pay you 1000 gold coins
if you never let her out of
your sight again.
One-eyed
Jack

One-eyed Jack put the
note in a bottle, sealed
it with a cork and threw
it into the sea.

Chapter 5
Polly Comes Home

Bottle ahoy!

Pirate Percy read the note.

"Polly's coming home!" he whooped.

His pirates were very pleased for him.

"And One-eyed Jack is giving us *1000 gold pieces*! We're going to be rich!" he shouted. His pirates jumped for joy.

Pirate Percy loved having Polly back home again. She nestled into his shoulder and squawked.

Pieces of eight, pieces of eight!

One-eyed Jack found a goldfish to keep him company.
It didn't bite. It didn't make a mess. But best of all,

it didn't make any noise!